Lucien Bély
Professor at the Sorbonne

D0128320

MONT SAINT-MICHEL

Photographs

Hervé Champollion

Hervé Champollion is represented by the TOP-RAPHO, Paris

Translation: Paul Williams, Angela Moyon, 5/5
Back cover:
Top, left: E. Cattin ; bottom, right: B. Demée

ÉDITIONS OUEST-FRANCE

Aerial view of the Mont Saint-Michel:
Western part of the abbey. Photo Richard Nourry.

© 1999 Édilarge S.A. - Éditions Ouest-France, Rennes

SUMMARY

Saint Michel, the monk Gelduin and the devil, Ms 50, F1, Saint Clement.
Reconnaissances. Scriptorium of the Mont Saint-Michel, after 966. Photo: Avranches Library.

THE HISTORY OF MONT SAINT-MICHEL

The story of the rock, the forest and the sea.

Try to imagine the Mont Saint-Michel before anything was built on it. It was a two hundred and fifty foot high rock with sheer sides. The granite which it is made up of, is a very hard rock which, for thousands of years, has resisted erosion from wind and water. This is the reason why this rock, together with one or two others, stands out in what is generally low-lying country.

Around the rock was forest, which may have been called Scissy Forest. It has now disappeared, for the sea over the years engulfed it. Some tree trunks have actually been found buried in the sand. According to legend, an enormous tidal wave swept over the area, transforming it completely at the beginning of the 8th century when Bishop Aubert dedicated the rock to Saint Michael. Ever since then, it has been an island just like the rock next to it, which is known as Tombelaine.

The vision of Saint Aubert. MS 210 F 4 back (detail), Chartulary of the Mont Saint-Michel Scriptorium of the Mont Saint-Michel, 1154-1158.
Photo: Avranches Library

The tide in the bay where the rock stands, is among the strongest in the world. The difference in depth of water between low and high tide in the same place is around forty feet. The beaches are almost completely flat. The sea has to come in many miles in just a few hours before reaching high water mark. The sea comes in at an amazing speed. It can be as fast as a horse at the gallop, and can prove quite dangerous for people fishing or walking on the beach.

Three rivers flow out onto the shore: the Sée, the Sélune and the Couesnon. The latter marks the boundary between Brittany and Normandy, for as the old saying goes: "The Couesnon's act of folly left the Mont in Normandy". The grey silt, known locally as "tangue", gives delicate colouring to the landscape. Grass grows on those areas of the sandy shore which are no longer covered at high tide. The sheep that graze there are known locally as "pré-salés" (salt-meadow) sheep because of the salty tang in the grass.

In this land of sand, sky and sea was built an abbey in the style of a citadel, the overall height of which, including the church's steeple, is well over five hundred feet.

The Mont Saint-Michel, view from the north.
In the foreground: La Merveille, i.e. the gothic part of the abbey.

The history of Mont Saint-Michel

The hermits

As the Roman Empire declined, a new religion appeared: Christianity. Men who believed in one God and in his son, Jesus of Nazareth, were overrunning Europe. They swept aside Roman gods and the ancient gods who inhabited woods and pools of water. To escape from the company of their fellow men and from worldly pleasures, holy men, called hermits, lived in great poverty in lonely forests and deserted islands. The place which we now call Mont Saint-Michel was known in those days as Mont Tombe which meant literally "tomb on a hill". The rock no doubt attracted hermits, for Christians, perhaps from Ireland, had settled very early on around the bay and near Dol-de-Bretagne. A remarkable legend tells us how fishermen provided food for the hermits living on the Mont. Whenever a hermit went hungry, he lit a fire; the villagers saw the smoke and loaded up a donkey with provisions. God then guided it through what remained of the Forest of Scissy until it arrived safely at the holy man's refuge. One day a wolf devoured the innocent donkey and, as a punishment, God forced it to carry all the provisions from then on.

Meanwhile, the cult of Saint Michael was spreading from the East towards Gaul. Heavenly beings were the angels and the archangels Michael, Raphael and Gabriel. According to the Bible, when Lucifer, the fallen angel, compared himself with God, another angel stood up before him and shouted "Who is like God?", in other words Mi-ka-el, or Michael. God entrusted him to lead his army, for Michael is "Prince of the Heavenly Host". He wears a suit of armour or a long white tunic. He holds a sparkling sword or lance. In the Apocalypse, a book written by the Apostle, Saint John, a dragon with seven crowned heads and horns, and a tail that swept aside the stars, threatened the Virgin Mary and her Holy Child who had just been born.

The Salisbury breviary: The Mont Saint-Michel and its 15th century ramparts; the archangel watches over Aubert who greets the first pilgrims. Aubert strikes the rock with his bishop's staff and, like Moses, causes a spring to gush out. The first mass is celebrated in the new sanctuary.
Paris, BNF, ms latin 17294.

7

Saint Michel

Angels were present everywhere in the holy Bible, the servants, soldiers and messengers of God. Despite reluctance on behalf of the Fathers of the Fathers of the Christian church, this tradition was adapted to Christianity. A hierarchy was even established among the heavenly creatures: Michel is an «archangel», above the angels. As the remarkable Christians who were worshipped as saints after their death, archangel Michel became Saint Michel. Even though his attributes were those of a warrior, he also was the leader of souls. He also frequently embodied the forces of the earth, and was related to phenomena that fired the imagination, such as lightning, light, comets or strange places, like rocks lashed by the waves: the Mont-Saint-Michel, for instance.

The archangel Saint Michel fighting the dragon.

Michael and his angels fought this serpent from Satan and destroyed it.

Aubert dedicates the rock to saint Michel

The Archangel often appeared in Italy: in Rome near the castle which still bears the name Holy Angel, and at Monte Gargano, a rocky peninsular on the Adriatic Sea.

The town of Avranches, which is very close to the Mont, in the year 708 was ruled by a bishop called Aubert. One night, he saw Saint Michael in a dream. The archangel ordered him to make the rock that had just been surrounded by the sea, into a place of worship dedicated to him. Aubert did nothing about it, thinking his imagination had got the better of him. Saint Michael grew impatient with him, and when he appeared the third time, he poked a hole in Aubert's skull to make him believe. He caused many more miracles to take place, so as to convince the bishop and his followers. A bull that had been stolen, was found at the very top of the Mont, as Michael had predicted. One story has it that Aubert was to build his church as large as the area trodden on by the bull; according

to another story, it was to occupy the space left dry in the midst of the morning dew.

Aubert fulfilled Michael's wishes and despatched messengers to Monte Gargano in Italy. They bought back some sacred relics: a piece of the red cloak worn by the Archangel during one of his apparitions, and a fragment of the altar where he had placed his foot.

When they returned, Aubert began to construct the sanctuary. The builders received some divine assistance with their task. An old man who lived nearby was called by God to move a huge stone. Another story tells of how a small child simply touched it with his foot and pushed it over the edge. There was no drinking water on the rock, but miraculously a spring was discovered. This is now called Saint Aubert's spring.

As time went by, the rock began to be known as Mont Saint-Michel, and Aubert sent a few men to live there and pray to God and his Archangel.

The foundation of the abbey

The peace and prosperity brought by Charlemagne lasted a short while. Men from the North, or Normans, came and pillaged the coast every year. Their fast, slender boats, known as drakkars, brought widespread terror. Above all else, they pillaged sanctuaries where there were objects of gold for the glory of God. The Mont had its fair share of these dreadful expeditions. In the

end, the Normans came and settled, and the king of the Franks recognised one of their chiefs, Rolf le Marcheur, or Rollon, as the "Duke of Normandy". In exchange, the formidable warrior became a Christian along with all his soldiers, and from then on protected all those in God's service.

Rollon and his descendants encouraged the rebuilding of important sanctuaries. But these new converts to the faith had high standards. Duke Richard reproached the priests who lived on the Mont for their immoral and impious behaviour. He threw them out and replaced them in 966 with submissive and humble monks from Flanders

A Benedictine monk in prayer.
MS 213, F229,
History of the Mont Saint-Michel, Scriptorium of the Mont Saint Michel, 14th-16th centuries.
Photo Avranches Library.

The Benedictines

Saint Benoît founded a monastery on the Mont-Cassin in the 6th century, and wrote a "Principle" to organise the lives of those who wanted to devote theirs to the prayer and glorification of God. He adapted the practises of the hermits in the Orient to the world of the Occident. In the 8th century, saint Benoît d'Aniane renewed the Benedictine discipline. The Principle of saint Benoît was spread further, for it was pragmatic and applicable to the activities of the monks. It ordered a strict spiritual life, but was supple with material life, and granted men or women the right to live as a community. In 910, the Benedictine abbey of Cluny was established in Burgundy: it was soon to be at the head of a network of monasteries that covered most of Europe. In 1958, saint Benoît was declared "father of Europe and patron of the Occident".

Saint Michel and the dragon, the Mont Saint-Michel, miniature from the **Très Riches Heures du duc de Berry,** beginning of the 15th century (ms 65/1284, fol. 195 r°), Chantilly, Condé Museum.
Photo Giraudon.

Normandy

The Normans were raiders and pagans; nonetheless, they settled on the Channel's coastline and became Christian converts. This meant that a severe domination was established, the submission to the newcomers of the populations that already resided in these areas, the construction of a strong State. Monks flowed to Normandy, drawn by the dukes' new-found piety: a true land of mission was opening itself to them, and the dukes of Normandy wisely relied on abbots and Benedictine monks like those of the Mont-Saint-Michel. Even if the duke admitted the authority of his weak neighbour, king of Francie or France, the duchy remained truly independent for a long time, in particular once it joined forces with kingdom of England. Later, in 1214, the victory of Bouvines saw Normandy become a province of the French kingdom.

The Mont Saint Michel
In the foreground, the Saint-Aubert chapel.

guided by a man of noble family called Maynard. These eleven monks adopted the rule of Saint Benedict which required them to organise their lives according to the principles of poverty, chastity and obedience. The abbey had become a Benedictine abbey.

The monk's leader was the abbot, or "father" of the community. He administered all the possessions of the monastery, encouraged the cult of Saint Michael, and received visitors. Theoretically, the monks themselves elected their own superior, but in practice, the Duke of Normandy, as protector of the abbey, persisted in selecting his own candidate for a long time.

This would become the cause for many quarrels and conflicts. Some abbots, however, owing to their faith, their authority and their generosity, won their surroundings' admiration: Bernard du Bec, for instance. He imposed misbehaving monks solitary retreats on the Tombelaine island; he let an ill knight wear the Benedictine dress on his death bed. This abbot thus increased the abbey's prestige and power.

The Romanesque age

The monk's vocation was to pray, both for themselves and for all men. Behind the high walls of the monastery, in the "enclosure", they avoided, as far as they could, all worldly temptations and violence. Their day was divided into eight hours: Matins at daybreak, Lauds, Prime, Terce, Sext around midday, Nones, Vespers, and Compline at the

end of the day. Each of these hours was accompanied by prayers which were read out of "books of hours", or breviaries.

Knights, in feudal times, engaged themselves in the profession of arms. But as death grew near, they turned to the abbeys. A captain, Néel de Saint-Sauveur, sought refuge and peace on the Mont Saint-Michel. Many warriors too asked to be buried in holy ground near sanctuaries.

When the old buildings were no longer big enough, the abbey, because of its wealth, was able to expand. An immense church was built at the top of the rock, to serve as a grandiose setting for prayer. Building techniques had progressed in Normandy. The style of architecture that later came to be known as Romanesque, was at its height. With the help of strong supporting pillars and huge arches to support beams and domes, the walls could be built extremely high. Two high towers, now no longer there, used to set off the façade of the church. To support this church, crypts, or subterranean chapels, were built along the contours of the rock. Their vaults, such as the one in the Saint-Martin crypt, were works of art. The very weight of the stones and the ingenious stonework ensured that the building was sound. The monks liked to pray in the half-light of the crypts. The living quarters, known as the "conventuels", occupied three floors in the northern part of the abbey. The dormitory (now the sacristy) was near the church; below was the monks' promenade that has often

been transformed over the ages; finally, near the north-west door, was the so-called Aquilon room, built in the Romanesque style, where pilgrims were received.

Famous pilgrims

Very soon, famous pilgrims came to the Mont Saint-Michel to implore the Archangel's protection. Richard II, Duke of Normandy, married Judith of Brittany there in the presence of the nobility of both provinces. On that occasion, he offered the abbey some churches, mills, lands and forests. One Duke of Brittany placed on the altar, property deeds of lands which he was making over to the monastery. These numerous gifts amounted to a vast amount of property all around the Bay. Peasants, that worked on these lands, regularly transported to the island, either by boat or on carts at low tide, part of their harvests. In exchange they received protection and justice.

The abbot, in his turn, honoured the protectors of the abbey. When Duke William completed the conquest of England, the superior of the Mont sent six ships and four monks to salute the new king. The finest of all the abbots was Robert de Thorigny who had been a skilful member of the Court of the Plantagenet King,

William the Conqueror

Military adventures and maritime expeditions remained long to the liking of the Normans. Some took part in the Crusade, others settled in Sicily, but they essentially devoted themselves to the conquest of England. Duke Roberts' bastard son succeeded in establishing himself in Normandy, then, at the death of Edward the Confessor, king of England, he ordered that ships be built in ten months, that he then unleashed across the Channel to vanquish his English rival Harold, in Hastings, in the year 1066. William "the Conqueror" became king of England. For four hundred years, the histories of Normandy and England were connected. As the same nobility then ruled both countries, Norman monks were also summoned to advise and assist the king in his new kingdom and lead the English Church.

Norman longships,
Scene 6 of the Bayeux tapestry,
11th century.
Printed with special permission from the city of Bayeux.

Cross section of the transept and the chancel of the abbey church.

Henry II, who reigned over England and a large part of France.

This abbot administered the abbey at the peak of its fortune. He welcomed there a whole line of magnificent princes. King Henry II, whom he served as counsellor, came and visited him, accompanied by King Louis VII of France, the Archbishop of Rouen, two cardinals who later became Popes, and five abbots. Their entrance into the abbey was an occasion for sumptuous ceremony. The entire community awaited the royal visitors on the shore at the entrance to the town with the Gospels, incense and holy water. All the bells rang out as the distinguished gathering made for the church.

Robert de Thorigny added to the community by recruiting a larger number of monks during his travels; he enriched the library, and finally had built, on the south-west side of the abbey, a huge hostel for pilgrims, which collapsed at the biginning of the 19th century. One the west side, he built his own quarters.

The miracles

Whenever some strange, fortuitous event occurred on the Mont, it was always attributed to the influence of Saint Michael. The monks built up a whole collection of these "miracles" which pilgrims and travellers passed down over the centuries.

One day, a blind woman stood in front of the Mont, and when her face turned towards it, she recovered her sight. "How beautiful it is to be able to see", she exclaimed and the name Beauvoir (beautiful to see) was given to the village where she was. Another woman, who was expecting a child, unwisely attempted to cross the shore. She suddenly felt the first birth pangs and fell to the sand. The tide was coming in, but a miracle took place and she was spared. When the fishermen found her safe and sound, her child had been born.

The men of the Middle Ages thought that the bones of saints had miraculous powers. The bones of Bishop Aubert, now Saint Aubert, had disappeared. A long time after the foundation of the abbey, a piece of music, that the monks thought had been sent from heaven, began to be heard. They started to look for it and questioned the nephew of one of the canons who had previously been expelled. Caskets were found hidden in the dormitory ceiling. A miraculous force caused the locks to open and inside were the Saint's relics. A parchment was found, that proved the authenticity of the bones.

Religious feasts

The men of the Middle Ages liked religious feasts. The architecture of the Mont, with its huge church, mysterious crypts and great stairways, lent itself well to splendid ceremonies.

There were frequent processions through the abbey. The abbot then, just like a bishop,

wore a mitre and carried a crook. The monks, instead of their severe, rough habits wore long, sleeveless cloaks known as albs. The whole monastery was lit up with candles. The relics in their reliquaries, and the Gospels, were taken among the pilgrims in the midst of clouds of incense. The procession came to a halt at special places where fervent prayers were said.

These ceremonies could turn into veritable theatrical shows. Monks played the parts of characters in the New Testament to help everyone understand the sacred texts, in the style of mystery plays held in front of cathedrals. In the 12th century, a monk from the Mont, who was a poet, wrote in the vernacular which all could understand (and not in Latin which was the language of the church), some verses which told the abbey's history and the miracles which had been wrought there. It was called the *Roman du Mont Saint-Michel* (The Story of the Mont Saint-Michel) and was the work of a monk who had all the qualities of a real minstrel.

These ceremonies were always accompanied by singing, the monks' one passion. The human voice enhanced prayer.

This plain song, or Gregorian chant, by virtue of its austerity and simplicity, was a form of worship in itself.

Finally, the reception of a new monk involved a moving ceremony. The young man's head was partly shaved: this was called the "tonsure", and was a symbol of his ecclesiastical calling. After one year's observation, he was allowed to take his vows in front of the whole community. The abbot helped him to put on a monk's habit to the accompaniment of songs of praise, and bestowed upon him a kiss of peace. For three days, he then prayed in the church. But after that, he was judged worthy to be a monk.

Miniature of the ***Livre d'heures*** by Peter 11, Duke of Brittany, 1450-1457, pilgrims arriving at the Mont Saint-Michel
Paris, BNF, ms latin 1159, fol. 160 v°.

The Saint-Aubert chapel.

The gothic cloisters at the top of the abbey, Photo Richard Nourry.

The Gothic art

New technologies met the monks' requirements, who desired space, light and beauty. An evolution had left its' mark in architecture. The semi-circular vault had been preferred in the Romanic age, but was liable to warp, and would not suit very tall buildings. Soon, two intersecting semi-circular vaults were used to cover chapels: the groined vault was created. To reinforce the groins, stone cutters then traced diagonal ribs: these created the rib vault. Soon, by skilfully balancing the weight of the vaults and the strength of the external buttresses, by using a framework of columns and arches, architects could raise walls of great height, carry roofing to impressive heights and open wide bays in walls without weakening them. To gain stability, the canted arch was often used. This is how the ogival art was elaborated, art that the following centuries despised by calling it "gothic", meaning barbaric.

The marvel

At the beginning of the 13th century, the great Anglo-Norman kingdom broke up. The King of France, Philippe-Auguste, took Normandy after a number of bloody battles. In the meantime, Mont Saint-Michel was besieged by an ally of the French King. The town and the abbey were in part destroyed by fire. In order to be pardoned and to convert the monastery to his cause, Philippe-Auguste sent a large amount of gold there, for it was necessary to rebuild.

A new art form, known later as "Gothic", was beginning to gain a hold. It was the age of the cathedral. The "ogival" arch led to the construction of particularly spacious and high buildings. The abbots of the Mont and their architects concentrated on the monk's living quarters. This was how the "Merveille", or "Marvel", came to be built on the north side. It was a masterpiece of Gothic architecture. The Romanesque buildings were no longer large enough to accommodate the monks, whose numbers had increased, for they too were changing with the times and were concerned with more comfort and beauty to suit their life style.

The architects were certainly ambitious to dare to build such a high and vast building on this steep rock. Enormous buttresses were built on the outside to shore up the Marvel. But, at the same time, as the construction got higher, it had to become less and less massive, so as to forestall any possibility of collapse — a not infrequent occurence in the history of the Mont. The almonry and the store house on the bottom floor had very thick walls and strong vaults; on the second floor, the Guests' room and the Knights' room had columns and ogival arches to support the third floor which contained the refectory and the cloister.

The stones arrived by sea at high tide from the Chausey Islands off the Mont. Stone-masons carved the granite into the correct shape. Sometimes they decorated it. Then with the help of ropes, pulleys or hoists such as the one that can still be seen at the Mont, the materials were hoisted up the scaffolding. When everything was assembled, the wooden supporting frames were removed.

The life of the monks

From now on, the monks spent most of their time in the Marvel. Poor pilgrims were welcomed in the almonry, rich ones on the floor above, in the Guests' room. Both places were near the entrance which, like it is today, was to the east, and not to the north-west as in the Romanesque era. The community kept well out of the way on the higher floors of the Marvel, near the church.

The thick walls of the refectory were pierced with long narrow windows that let in plenty of light, and supported a fine wooden "cradle" vault. Meals took place in silence while one monk read sacred texts from a pulpit situated on the south wall. The cloister, suspended in mid-air between sea and sky, was for talking a stroll, for meditation and conversation. The arcades are supported on fine columns of purple stone. Above the columns, the soft, white limestone of Caen has been carved into flowers and leaves. These carvings are an admirable example of Norman decorative art.

Before the introduction of printing, the only way of preserving and reproducing a text was to copy it by hand. This was done by the monks, who went to great pains to decorate and beautify manuscripts. This was the art of illumination. Colours and designs were used to illuminate and illustrate individual letters. The Mont was known as the "city of books", for there were so many fine works in its library. The monks were not only interested in sacred texts and prayers, but also the works of Antiquity. The "chauffoir", or hot room, was the place where the monks conducted this meticulous work, as well as everything else. This room, that was later called the "Knights'" room, shows only too well that the monk's main enemy was the dank cold that came from the sea and the mist. They fought against it by lighting huge fires, and using tapestries and furs for insulation. Actually, many monks would rather live in priories, that were small dependencies of the abbey, on dry ground.

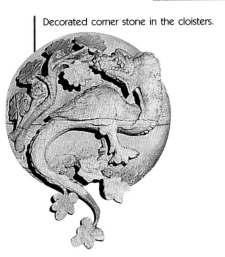

Decorated corner stone in the cloisters.

Cloisters of the Mont Saint-Michel, by Emmanuel Lansyer, 1881.
© Quimper Museum of Fine Arts.

Pilgrimages

In the Middle Ages, it was considered a duty to go on a pilgrimage. The richest or the bravest went to the Holy Land, Rome or Compostella. Others had to be content with a sanctuary that was nearer home. The Mont Saint-Michel, of course, was a great Norman centre of pilgrimage, but it also attracted pilgrims from all over France and all of western Christendom. Christians went there to pray to the Archangel for their sins to be forgiven and for all their hopes to come true. Ill people especially hoped that a miracle would give them back their health, as used to happen in the legends emanating from the Mont.

Sometimes God's calling was sudden and inexplicable : a man could set off for the Mont in the middle of shoeing a horse, leaving the job unfinished. In 1333, the entire population of a village suddenly left for the Mont, forcing their parish priest to go with them and say Mass there.

A pilgrim on his way to the Mont was called a "miquelot". Like all other pilgrims, he was recognisable by his leather sack that was carried over his right shoulder, and by his roughly hewn staff. He would also have

Saint Michel.
Pilgrimage sign in lead and tin
15th century, probably
from the Mont Saint-Michel,
found in the Seine,
Paris.
Musée National
du Moyen Age
Thermes
et hôtel
de Cluny.
© Photo
R.M.N.

shells, the very symbols of a pilgrimage, stitched to his clothing.

A pilgrim could expect help and respect on his journey. He was given shelter for the night in special inns right the way along the roads leading to the Mont. These roads were called "the ways of Paradise".

He was threatened by many a danger, among them illness and fatigue. When he finally caught sight of the famous shape of the Mont he shouted out "Montjoie", Mount Joy, in this great relief.

However, he now still needed to cross the strand, over a distance of one or two miles; and the quicksands were very dangerous, as was the sudden tide that could swallow him up. Vagabonds would also try to mislead credulous pilgrims into the mist, to steal their purse.

The arrival of a pilgrimage at the Mont Saint-Michel in the beginning of the century.
Avranches Library postcard collection.

Pilgrimage to the Mont Saint-Michel.
Photo Yvon Boëlle.

A religious service.
Photo Bertrand Demée.

Miquelots at the Mont

All kinds came to the Mont: invalids, pilgrims and wrong-doers mixed together, and all languages and dialects could be heard. Everyone was full of hope. Some wanted to repeat the experience of Norgod, Bishop of Avranches, who saw a bright light come down to the rock thereby revealing the presence of Saint Michael. Others even tried to spend the night in the dark church, only to give up after one of them was slapped by the invisible hand of God.

The pilgrim took part in the religious festivals. He tried to touch the reliquaries which contained the precious relics,

the most curious of which were a tiny sword and shield that the archangel is said to have used to kill a dragon, and that had

Greeting retirees at the Mont Saint-Michel. Photo Bertrand Demée.

been brought by some miraculous means from a far-off country. The faithful pilgrim was also expected to make offerings: King Philip the Fair gave a statue covered in gold; the poor made do with a piece of wax that went towards lighting the chapels.

The town nestling at the foot of the abbey welcomed the travellers. They dined in the taverns and slept in the hostelries. But important visitors. were received by the abbot in the very large and bright Guests' room. Food was prepared in the two enormous hearths that were hidden from the rest of the room by sumptuous tapestries. Lavatories were installed in the north wall. The reception room with its elegant columns was richly adorned. Beneath it, however, near the entrance to the Gothic abbey, was the simple and aus-

A monk today.
Photo Bertrand Demée.

tere almonry where the poorest people could get food.

Inside the city, shops sold souvenirs called pilgrimage "colours"; in particular, broaches made of silver or plain metal that represented Saint Michel or shells, but the pilgrims were mostly satisfied with a "cockle" or a "bucarde" that they picked up on the strand.

The life of the monks

The monks had elected the Mount due to its' isolation. Located as it was atop a rock surrounded by the sea and the sands, life was no mean feat, and one needs only to think of the difficulties that arose to supply the Mount with food or fresh water. Constructions too were fragile on this steep site, even if in time, the architects and stone cutters erected wonders as they took up natures' challenge. The beauty of this place, the monastery's great renown and the worship of Saint Michel attracted many pilgrims, which caused new problems. The pilgrims needed accommodation and food: the town located at the foot of the abbey and the monastic community shared these duties. Ceremonies needed also be offered to God, that would meet the believers' expectations.

MONT-St-MICHEL. - 4 - Fête Jubilaire - Journée des Bretons - 27 Juillet 1909 - L'arrivée du Pèlerinage

Cliché H. M.

"Bretons' Day" festival, 27th July 1909.
Collection of postcards, Avranches Library.

The abbey and the One Hundred Years' War

War broke out at the beginning of the 14th century between France and England, and took its toll together with the plague, which was then spreading throughout the whole of Christendom. It came to be called the "One Hundred Years' War".

After the serious French defeats at Poitiers and Crécy, King Charles V began to make a comeback with the help of his constable, Bertrand Duguesclin. This Breton knight was the captain of the Mont Saint-Michel. When he left France for Spain, he entrusted his wife, Tiphaine Raguenel, to the protection of Saint-Michael the Archangel. She lived in a house built at the top of the town, undertaking good works and practising the science of astrology which she was devoted to: she could read the future of the world in the movement of the stars.

On the occasion of one of his visits to the abbey, the mad King, Charles VI, made the abbot Pierre le Roi, who was an academic of some standing, into his counsellor. He immediately began to fortify the abbey. He defended the entrance by building towers, successive courtyards, and ramparts, thereby creating a veritable fort together with its "barbican". He completed the living quarters on the south side. These were reserved for the abbot and for the administrative and judiciary offices.

Normandy fell into English hands in 1415, after the French defeat at Agincourt. The province was then governed by the Duke of Bedford, the brother of the English King, who succeeded in winning over to his cause a number of leading Norman personalities. Among them was the abbot of the Mont, Robert Jolivet, Pierre le Roi's successor, who accepted to be counsellor to Bedford, and received, in exchange, all the property belonging to the monastery.

The monks refused to support their treacherous abbot. Some knights, who had been dispossessed of their lands, had sought refuge with them, and they stayed faithful to the French cause, the only defender of which was the Dauphin Charles, who was

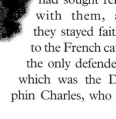

The Mont Saint-Michel, view from the south east.

later to become Charles VII, the so-called "King of Bourges".

The Romanesque chancel at the Mont collapsed and, because of the war, it was impossible to reconstruct it. One of the Mont's captains died in combat; the small island of Tombelaine fell into English hands; and, as a sinister omen of things to come, the river Couesnon changed course after an unusually high tide.

The shepherd lads and lasses

During these troubled times in the first half of the XIVth century, a strange phenomenon occured. Despite all the dangers involved, children began to go on pilgrimage to the Mont Saint-Michel. They were called the "shepherd lads and lasses" in popular ballads and tales. A chronicle from the town of Cologne in Germany contains a description of these great child crusades: "That year, there was a great pilgrimage to the Mont Saint-Michel in Normandy, a pilgrimage that lasted about two years and which was made up of small children of eight, nine, ten and twelve years of age, that came from all the towns and villages of Germany and Belgium, and other countries too". They gathered together in large numbers, abandonning their parents, and marched along, two by two, in procession. At the head of the column were students bearing effigies of Saint Michael. Children from the same area grouped together behind their own standard, which was decorated with the coats of arms of their local gentry. These children inspired pity, for they had left their homes against the wishes of their parents and without any money for the journey. Nevertheless, they remained in good health, for all along the road they were given food and drink in sufficient quantities. When they arrived at the Mont Saint-Michel, they offered their standards to the Archangel.

The procession grew in size on the way, as it was completed by elderly people, valets and servants of both genders...". These pugnacious and undisciplined crowds fascinated their contemporaries: young men had no qualms about leaving their families, their town, their country. But these pilgrimages worried the grave clergymen, who saw in them a cause of disorder and difficulties to come.

They lasted a long time, since a man of letters of the 18th century, rétif de la Bretonne, quoted a popular chorus:

Jacquot has gone on a pilgrimage to Saint-Michel, may he be guided on his journey by Raphaël,
This is where we kept
the white sheep,
Jacquot is going by the trembling bridge to get his pardon.

The Hundred Years' War

This conflict arose between Edward III, king of England, and Philippe VI de Valois, king of France, because the former was claiming the crown of France, as he was, by his mother, the grandson of Philippe le Bel. Edward had been set aside, especially due to the fact that he was English, but also in the name of a tradition that excluded women and their lineage from the royal inheritance - this rule was given the name "Salic law", derived from the name of the Salian Francs. This measure served to avoid that a princess gave the kingdom of France to her husband, and was a guarantee of the country's independence and identity. The so-called Hundred Years' War lasted for over one hundred years. It was not an all-out war: it was interrupted by numerous truces, and even happy periods. However, the military reality's extreme weight rested long on the population's shoulders.

Tombelaine Castle, fantastic vision based on a drawing founded in the Tower of London.
Collection of postcards, Avranches Library.

11. - Tombelaine, d'après un dessin trouvé à la Tour de Londres

The fortifications

The Hundred Years' War
led to protect the Mount's town,
that was surrounded by ramparts,
and the abbey, that now
resembled a citadel. But the art
of war had evolved. The use of
gunpowder had given birth to
heavy artillery, and, faced with
cannons, round towers were
very fragile, as were high walls.
Fortifications evolved little
by little, even if historians like to
speak of a military revolution.
The Boucle du Mont tower
is looked upon as one of the
first standing testimonies of this
evolution: instead of being round,
it was a polygon-shaped,
bastion-type construction, that
heralded Vauban's very skilful
creations in the 17th century.

The Arcade Tower.

The siege of the Mont

The beginning of the 15th century was a critical period for the Mont Saint-Michel.

The English decided to storm this stronghold which dared to stand up to them. A citadel that was defended both by its ramparts and by the sea was impregnable. It had to be surrounded and obliged to give itself up through famine and lack of water.

The siege began in 1424. Numerous troops took up positions around the Bay. A small wooden fort called the "bastille" was constructed at Ardevon, in front of the Mont, as a refuge in the event of an attack, and in order to keep a watch over the shore. Finally, a flotilla arrived to complete the blockade, from the sea.

Some Breton noblemen commanded an expedition from Saint-Malo and skilfully attacked the English ships and managed to disperse them. This naval victory enabled the Mont to receive provisions by sea. The siege had failed utterly and the citadel had not surrendered. For the first time in a long while, the

French were able to recover their confidence. It seemed that the Archangel himself had made this victory possible, and his cult won all the more prestige. This is why Saint Michael was among those who appeared to Joan of Arc. He told her: "I am Michael, the protector of France. Arise, and go to help the King of France". And he guided the shepherd girl from Lorraine through her great adventures.

Charles VII put a very able captain, called Louis d'Estouteville, in charge of the Mont's garrison. He set about putting an end to the squabbles, schemings, pillaging and debauchery that were now common in the abbey, and had been introduced by rough, coarse soldiers who knew no better. Because he tightened up discipline in this way, the citadel was able to withstand the last attack by the English in 1433. A fire broke out in the town, destroying the wooden houses and damaging the ramparts. The English tried to take advantage of this by coming in large numbers with terrible war engines which succeeded in breaching the walls. For a while, they thought they had taken the town, but the garrison held on, and, in the end, the English were forced to with-draw. The shore was strewn with the dead, and the knights

The English bombards.

from the Mont retrieved two enormous cannons which were set up at the entrance to the town where they can still be seen.

The knights of Saint Michel

The King at the end of the Middle Ages, Louis XI, was an able but cruel monarch. He was very devout, and even superstitious. He loved pilgrimages, which is why he twice visited the sanctuary which symbolised the French victory over the English.

It was this that made him think of creating the Order of the Knights of Saint Michael, with the Archangel as its first member. The Duke of Burgundy, who was a great enemy of the King, already had the Knights of the Golden Fleece. But the Knights of Saint Michael were the King's own creation and were chosen from among the finest noblemen of the kingdom. They received a necklace of golden shells on which hung a medal which depicted Michael slaying the dragon, and had written on it the motto of the Order: *"Immensi terror oceani"* (the terror of the immense ocean).

The dignitaries wore white damask robes and a red velvet headdress. They took part in splendid ceremonies presided over by the King at the chapel of Saint Michael in the heart of Paris.

The King had another idea which was nothing short of lugubrious. He ordered a wood and metal cage to be suspended from the ceiling at the Mont. Every time the prisoner inside moved, the whole

Reconstitution, d'après un document du xviiiᵉ siècle, de la Cage du Mont-Saint-Michel placée par Louis XI, dans l'ancienne Officialité. Après un an de détention, Victor de la Cassagne expira dans cette cage, le 27 Août 1746. Une odieuse légende dit qu'il y fut dévoré par les rats ; l'histoire démontre qu'il se laissa mourir de faim. Cette cage, de bois et de fer, servait aussi de chambre de punition pour les Exilés, c'est-à-dire pour les prisonniers détenus par ordre du Roi. Dimensions approximatives : longueur 2ᵐ88, largeur, 2ᵐ24, hauteur 2ᵐ56 ; porte sur le côté droit.
(Extrait de l'ouvrage : *Les Prisons du Mont-Saint Michel, de 1425 à 1864*, par Etienne DUPONT ; Paris, PERRIN, éditeur, Librairie Académique).

The iron stairwell, reconstruction based on a 18th century document of the stairwell of the Mont Saint-Michel that Louis XI had built in the former religious court house. Photo Avranches Library.

contraption began to rock. Being in this confined space in the freezing and lonely old abbey, was just like being in Hell. For centuries, political prisoners who had offended the King or his servants, were locked away there. Some were left for years at the mercy of the rats; some ended up going mad.

The last constructions

Captain d'Estouteville had strengthened the abbey's defences. The town, which had always been threatened in war, had been encircled by ramparts and strong towers such as the Roy, Cholet, Beatrix and Arcade towers. With all its cannons, machicolations through which various objects could be dropped in defence, and watchtowers which commanded a view over the shores, the Mont Saint-Michel had become one of the

The ramparts of the Mont Saint-Michel and the north tower.

Model of the
Mont Saint-Michel,
1701. Side view
of the terrace
and facade of the
abbey church.
Paris, Musée
des Plans-Reliefs.
Photo Dephti.

the "commendam" system, which involved the abbot residing outside his community while receiving the greater part of their revenue.

From that time on, the King handed over numerous abbeys to important people whom he wanted to honour or reward.

The cardinal's prestige, the influence he exerted upon the king and the pope facilitated the church's reconstruction. A crypt called the crypt "of the mighty pillars" supported the new construction, that would only be finished in the beginning of the 16th century. The tall and slender choir was lit by tall windows and an open gallery, whose sculptures were very delicate. To support the construction at the rock's summit, flying buttresses were elevated on the outside, to serve as stone "stays". This chevet was decorated with "pinnacles", that is fine pyramids adorned with flowers. Owing to its' richness and profusion, this art was named the "flamboyant" style. A "lace stairway", a suggestive name indeed, enabled the ascent, through this granite forest, to the rooftops, from where the eye could embrace the whole of the bay.

The lace stairway.

strongest forts of its day. A lot of progress had been made during the long war in the art of attack and self-defence.

Abbot Jolivet had died at Rouen in the midst of the English whom he had served well. Louis d'Estouteville had appointed his brother, Guillaume, as abbot of the Mont. This man was a prince of the Church, a cardinal. He wasn't a monk but a priest. His many important commitments prevented him from devoting all his time to the monastery, which he left in the hands of the prior. Thus started

The wars of Religion

At the beginning of the 16th century, one of the king's lieutenants completed the defences of the town. From now on, the entrance to the town was well protected by the Avancée, Boulevard and Roy gates, which were reinforced by the addition of a moat, drawbridge and portcullis.

Throughout the century, the Kings of France visited the famous abbey, and François 1st was received there with great pomp. But the Wars of Religion threw the kingdom into confusion, and the Mont was caught up in a whirlwind of battles and massacres.

The religious wars

In the 16th century, the catholic church was challenged, and a new denomination gained ground, first with Luther, then with Calvin: Protestantism. This spread across France, and conversions steadily became more frequent. The French monarchy attempted to halt its' progression - in vain. After Henri II's death, his sons followed one another on the throne: François II, Charles IX then Henri III, and queen mother Catherine de Médicis was given the opportunity to exert great influence on the government. But already Catholics and Protestants were at war, and divisions even existed in each camp. In 1572, Charles IX ordered that the Protestant gentlemen in Paris at the time be massacred, but this blew on the embers of the civil war. It grew to a new dimension when it appeared that the successor of Henri III de Valois would be his distant cousin Henri de Bourbon, who was a Protestant. For Henri IV to earn recognition as the king of France required him to be converted to Catholicism, to reconquer his kingdom and meet a religious compromise, that was to be the Edict of Nantes.

The Protestants tried to capture this Catholic strong-hold. Since it was reputed to be impregnable, Captain Le Touchet endeavoured, in 1577, to take it through cunning. Men

Plate from
Atlas curieux
by Nicolas de Fer,
1705, Oparius. Paris,
musée des Plans-Reliefs.
Photo Dephti.

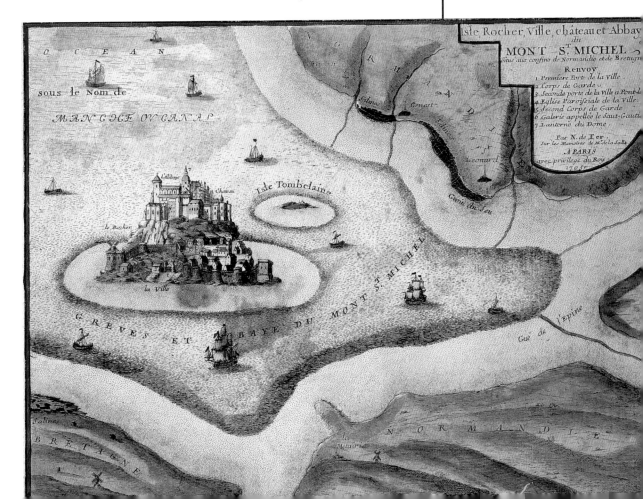

Entrance to the dungeon.
Photo Richard Nourry.

The prisoners of the Mount

The idea of locking men in to punish them dawned slowly. For a long time, the sentence delivered for a crime or an offence was death, mutilation, public humiliation or a fine. When the judges didn't know what verdict to deliver, or when the monarchic government did not want a suspect to be tried publicly, it was chosen to keep him imprisoned. As no establishment had been foreseen for this, citadels like la Bastille, in Paris, or fortified monasteries, such as the Mont-Saint-Michel were resorted to. In the first case, the garrison was responsible for keeping watch over the prisoners, in the second case, these duties were taken over by the monastic community. This partly explains why the prisoners of the Mount were imprudent men of letters or debauched individuals, of whom the families wanted to be rid. When the French Revolution scattered the monks, the Mount remained in use as a prison.

disguised as pilgrims hid their weapons and managed to get within the walls. They won over the soldiers watching the abbey gates by offering them wine, and then took up their positions on the Saut-Gauthier to await reinforcements. A novice (future monk) from the abbey realised what they were up to and gave the alarm. The monk alerted the townspeople at the foot of the monastery. When they realised they had been discovered, the false pilgrims tried to bluff their way out by shouting "the town has been taken", but the inhabitants took up their arms to help the monks. Captain Le Touchet, who was just arriving with his horsemen, had to turn back, leaving his companions to surrender.

Another stratagem was used later by members of the formidable Montgomery family. Men disguised as women and fishermen approached the Mont. The guards at the town gate grew suspicious and killed them all in cold blood. The Huguenot troops appeared from no-where and took the town. But the abbey continued to resist. The military governor was away from the Mont at the time, but as soon as he received news of what was happening, he gathered some men and rushed back. They hoisted themselves up, with the help of ropes, to the ramparts above the occupied town and started a counter-offensive. The Protestants, caught between two lines of fire,

were defeated, and all the prisoners were locked up on Tombelaine Island.

The abbey in ruins

Monastic life was on the wane. The monks began to abandon their abbey: some of them preferred to live in the taverns. They were no longer respected. The abbots, such as Abbot de Guise or Cardinal de Montmorency, were selected by the King from amongst the finest nobility. But they no longer visited the Mont: they were quite content to collect some of its revenue. An unexpected revival took place when new Benedictines, the Maurists, took it over. These learned men were devoted to the history of the Mont, which they studied from the collection of manuscripts that had been built up over the ages.

Excursion to the Mont Saint-Michel, poster produced by the Chemins de fer de l'Ouest (Western Railways), 1895. Conservatoire de l'Affiche de Locronan.

The buildings were badly maintained and virtually falling into ruin. Both the high towers and three supporting arches in the church collapsed. They were not rebuilt in their original style but replaced in 1780 by a very simple Classical façade.

Meanwhile, the abbey was transformed into a prison and became the "sea Bastille". Writs were issued by the King to banish to the island without fair trial, debauched aristocrats, corrupt priests and political opponents. The worst of them were shut up in dank, dark dungeons, or, indeed, in Louis XI's famous cage. In 1788, the duke of Orléans' sons came to visit the Mont Saint-Michel; they were guided by their governess, a famous novelist and teacher, Madame de Genlis. The eldest son, Philippe, became, King Louis-Philippe the first, in 1830. During their supper, prisoners were introduced, who told their extraordinary adventures. On the following day, the young prices visited the crypts and dungeons. They beheld the cage, this "barbaric monument", asked to hear its' story, and then demanded that it be destroyed. A Swiss soldier, who earned money by showing visitors this cage, was given a large tip as a compensation. In the children's presence, the cage's door was removed.

Tombelaine island

Tombelaine means «small tomb». This island, similarly to the Mont, is granite rock that was spared by erosion from the sea. Nowadays, this site is deserted; it was however, a long time ago, a modest replica of the great nearby abbey. A chapel and a priory had been constructed on it. Monks went to retire to the island, and a Venetian scholar worked there. Little by little, this site also became a citadel. The English took hold of it during the Hundred year war, and from there, became a threat to the Mont's garrison. In the 17th century, this castle belonged to Fouquet, and when the superintendent fell into disgrace, Louis XIV had the fortifications razed to the ground. Tombelaine, the island on which legends say that Hélène, King Arthur's bride, had died, disappeared from History.

The writers and the Mount

Writers expressed the impressions they felt when facing the Mont-Saint-Michel. The marquess of Sévigné, in 1689, wrote these lines to her daughter: "From my chamber, Il could see the sea and the Mont-Saint-Michel, a Mount so majestic, that you beheld in all its' pride, and who witnessed you to be so beautiful..." Victor Hugo recalled, in Ninety-three this "immense triangle, black in colour, with a cathedral for a tiara and a fortress for an armour", the Mount, "which is to the Ocean what Kheops is to the desert...". Théophile Gautier described it in the mist as "an immense erratic block, the remains of some antediluvian commotion, standing in the centre of this flat immensity, uniformly tinted with grey". Jules Michelet, in The Sea, beheld "a vast plain as white ashes, forever lonely, equivocal sand whose deceiving smoothness is the most dangerous of traps. It is the dry land and is the dry land no more, it is the sea and is the sea no more". Guy de Maupassant wrote that the abbey, "grown far away, far from the dry land, like a fantastic manor, as bewildering as a palace of dreams", was unbelievably strange and beautiful. Maurice Barrès saw the Mount rise "as a miracle out above quicksands".

The resurrection of the Mount

The French revolution scattered the last monks, but the Mont Saint-Michel remained a prison. The abbey was now but a «convict house», eerie and frightening After every riot or every failed revolution, new political prisoners were sent to it. Victor Hugo evoked the tragic fate of those men: "All around us, as far as the eye can see, infinite space, the blue horizon of the sea, the green horizon of the land, clouds, air, liberty, birds wheeling, ships at full sail; and then suddenly, over the top of the old wall above our heads, the pale face of a prisoner".

A few succeeded in escaping, such as the painter Colombat. He had found an old nail up during a fire in the abbey. He dug a hole in the wall. An accomplice sent him a rope, concealed in a loaf of bread. A night, between two patrols, he let himself slip down the rope, to the base of the walls. He was free, and his escape made him famous from one day to the following. Another famous prisoner, Barbès, attempted to copy him, but, shaken by wind and blinded by fog, he let the rope go, and merely earned himself a broken leg. The garrison was then alerted, and he was caught again.

The abbey was rediscovered by visitors and Romantic writers during the 19th century. They admired the extraordina-

20th lithograph showing the Mont Saint-Michel at high tide.
Avranches Museum.
Photo Paul Hay.

The Mont Saint-Michel, view from the Moidrey port,
by Paul Huard, circa 1840. Avranches Museum.

ry architecture. This was the birth of tourism. The prison was abolished under the Second Empire. In 1874, the Mont had become a "historic monument".

The Mont Saint-Michel rose again from its ruins. Restoration was undertaken, with extreme attention to detail. The Gothic steeple was rebuilt, thus giving the finishing touch to the famous silhouette rising above the sand. A single monk, and then a little community, came and revived the religious tradition. This abbey, which is also a citadel, bears witness to one thousand years of effort to please God, monks and pilgrims alike.

The Mont-Saint-Michel, by Eugène Isabey (1803-1886). Amiens, musée de Picardie. Photo Bulloz.

Local fisherman, reproduction of an old postcard, based on an original engraving by Lalaisse, 1852. Musée d'Avranches. Photo Avranches Library.

29

MONT-SAINT-MICHEL. — *Vue prise de la Digue*

**South side of the
Mont Saint-Michel.**
Horse-drawn carriages.
Collection of postcards,
Avranches Library.

**Tourists disembarking
at high tide.**
Collection of postcards,
Avranches Library.

94   MONT SAINT-MICHEL. — *L'Entrée du Mont à Marée haute*

ND Phot.

88 MONT SAINT-MICHEL. — *Arrivée du train sur la digue.* — ND. Phot.

Tram arriving
on the dyke.
Collection of postcards,
Avranches Library.

South side of the Mount
Saint-Michel,
departing train.
Collection of postcards,
Avranches Library.

Collection Germain fils aîné, St-Malo

5009. - MONT-SAINT-MICHEL
La Grande Rue - *G. F.*

Main Street at the beginning of the 20th century... Collection of postcards, Avranches Library.

A GUIDED TOUR OF MONT SAINT-MICHEL

Let us now look at the main features on any tour of the Mont. After passing through the town gates, the street rises up to the abbey. Our tour follows the traditional route but is only intended as a suggestion. Once you have seen the monastery, you should leave yourself time to stroll through the town and along the top of the town walls.

The town gates

... and today.

One of the major preoccupations of men in the Middle Ages was how to fortify the entrance to their town. Three huge gates were built to provide increased resistance to attack - the Forward, Boulevard and King's Gates. The third line of defence was the King's Gate (Porte du Roy) protected on the south side by the two great Arcade and King's Towers. A moat, drawbridge and portcullis made it even more difficult for attackers to enter the town. The coats-of-arms of the abbey, the town and the monarch, the symbols of the three levels of authority, were all carved on the gateway. The guards kept watch from the top of the parapet walk and were billetted in the King's Lodging. Leading up to this gate was the Boulevard and its gate, which were also designed in the 15th century. One hundred years later, the king's lieutenant completed the defensive system by building the Forward Gate (Porte de l'Avancée). The "bourgeoisie", i.e. the local population, were required to take turns to keep watch from this gate, which is flanked by the Bourgeois' Guardroom.

In 1434, fire raged through the town. The locals, who had already withstood a siege lasting several years, seemed to have lost all hope. The English launched an attack on the fortress, using an awesome display of weaponry, but they were repulsed. The victors carried off cannon known as michelettes or miquelettes. War had created its own means of destruction and the intense fire power of these bombards made it essential to strengthen the town walls and the entire system of defence.

Boulevard Gate.

Overhang Gate.

King's
Gate.

Abbey entrance:
the barbican
and castle fortress.

The entrance of the abbey

There is no doubt about it - the Abbey is a citadel. Although the steep sides of the rock made attack difficult, men throughout the ages have tried their best to give the monastery added protection. The Romanesque buildings already had a good system of defence. The Gothic "Marvel" with its three storeys, proud walls and mighty buttresses, gives every appearance of being impregnable.

With the first rumours of war came the continuation of military effort and, in the late 14th century, Pierre le Roi had the redoubt built. In front of it is a rectangular forework with crenelated walls, the barbican. It is flanked by two fine turrets, built to either side of the entrance itself. The staircase that leads up to the Guard-room was once closed off by a portcullis. The steps are particularly steep and

The inner town
with the abbey dwellings
in the background.

have been compared to an "abyss". Near the south postern gate (a fortified entrance) on the redoubt is an old tavern called "The Spinning Sow" (La Truie qui file).

After the long siege of the Mont by the English, Captain Louis d'Estouteville designed a first-class system of defence. All the ramparts were strengthened between 1425 and 1440, and the entire town was surrounded by

a wall. As firearms had become more reliable thanks to improvements made during various conflicts, the design allowed for their use here - they were, after all, an active means of defence. Gunports abound on the Mont, and the cannon were ready to repulse any attack.

The original entrance to the abbey lay to the north-east before being moved to the east. The gatehouse is on the ground floor,

and it contains the finest fire-place in the monastery, decorated with luxurious moulding. From 1364 onwards, visitors were required to leave their weapons here and, at the end of the 14th century, when the Mont became a citadel, the gatehouse was turned into the Guardroom. With its tall, storeyed vaulting, it opens onto the main inner staircase, the abbot's lodging and the Gothic almonry.

Shield tower.

From town to abbey:
view of the ramparts
from the great outer
staircase.
Photo Yvon Boëlle.

The *Great Outer Staircase* leads from the town to the Abbey.

In the Middle Ages, "entry" into a town or abbey involved grandiose ceremonial if the visitor was powerful and famous. It was a sacred act and was eventually subject to rules laid down by tradition. The king was received at the town gates, the Archbishop of Rouen at the top of the town, and the Bishop of Avranches at the entrance to the abbey itself. The entrance ceremony was a reflection of social hierarchy and, because of this, the architecture had to provide a majestic backdrop to the slow climb up the rock. The *Great Inner Staircase*, with its landings and wide steps, was an integral part of the ceremony.

It runs alongside the abbey lodgings, forming the "worldly" part of the abbey which is in permanent contact with visitors.

The staircase also had a defensive role. To reach the church, attackers would have to pass through here, along what

was, in fact, a ditch between two high walls. Monks or soldiers could defend it from the two fortified bridges connecting the lodgings to the interior of the church. The stone bridge with machicolations was built in the 15th century and its military function is quite obvious. The other bridge was built of timber and slate, in the 16th century. The Great Steps lead to the terrace called the Saut-Gauthier, that leads to the church's southern doors.

The great inner staircase.

The spire
and the archangel,
work by Frémiet.

Facade of the church.

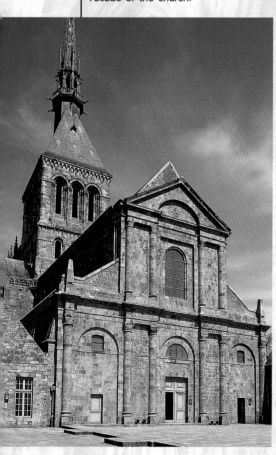

The abbey church

Building began on the church in the 11th century but the original construction was fragile and required alteration on several occasions over the years.

The west Front and the original layout

From the 16th to 19th centuries, the buildings fell into disrepair. The first three spans of the church were demolished in the 18th century. The Classical facade was completed in 1780. Its austerity and unobtrusiveness is particularly well-suited to the Mont. The Romanesque facade was also very plain. It was flanked by two towers that were reminiscent of the ones in Jumièges; they were built during the abbacy of Robert de Thorigny. One of them was demolished in the Middle Ages; the other one, the Clock Tower on the south side, survived until the fire in 1776. The first spans of the church were replaced by this west-facing platform called the "Plomb du Four", the "end of the nave". The platform looks westward towards the Isles Chausey which provided the granite for the buildings on the Mont. The present sacristy on the left of the West Front was originally the monks' dorter. It forms the upper storey of the Romanesque monastery buildings. The short distance separating it from the church enabled the monks to go to the sanctuary in the dark to *sing* Matins.

The belltower

Lightning struck the church tower on numerous occasions, setting fire to the fragile wooden construction. In the Gothic period, a tall spire was built, flanked by six small pyramidal towers. In the 17th century, an onion dome was erected and a platform was built onto it in the 18th century for the Chappe telegraph. Finally, the architect Petitgrand designed the present tower. Above its two "Romanesque" storeys is a Gothic spire which is a copy of the one on Notre-Dame cathedral in Paris. It is topped by a statue of St. Michael brandishing his lance as he slays the dragon – a piece of sculpture by Frémiet. And so Mont Saint-Michel acquired its final outline.

The arms of the abbey

This coat-of-arms surrounded by carved drapes was placed at the entrance to the church in the 18th century, behind the new West Front. The abbey's arms took many years to achieve their final form. In the 15th century, they consisted of three shells. They then became a "sprinkling of sable (i.e. black) shells bearing at their head (in a horizontal band) the fleur-de-lys of France". The abbey became a centre of pilgrimage very early on in its existence, as is shown by the shells which were the distinguishing mark of pilgrims all

along their route. The fleurs-de-lys, the symbol of the French monarchy, were then added to the arms. They proclaimed the King of France as the protector of the monastery and fortress. The crozier and mitre, which were sometimes added for decoration, showed the rank of the abbot who was "mitred and croziered" i.e. of equivalent rank to a bishop. Each abbot also had his own family coat-of-arms which he often included in the stained glass windows in the church.

The Romanesque nave (11th century)

Mediaeval architects brought a sense of movement into the church by breaking up the impression of length with arches and the appearance of height with upper storeys.

The nave originally had seven arches or spans, and was completed c. 1084. At that time, Norman architecture was in its heyday, thanks to the Abbot-Architect, William of Volpiano. The Normans only used vaulting in the "most sacred" parts of their church. In the nave, they were content with timber rafters, which had the advantage of forming a lighter barrel vault on the narrow surface of the rock.

The ceiling in the church may originally have been flat. The timber vaulting is thought to have been built in the 15th century.

The transept crossing was built in 1138 on the orders of Bernard du Bec. It has ogival vaulting, a precursor of things to come. When carving out the space for the bell in the late 19th century, the architect-in-charge, Petitgrand, totally restored this section with its four pillars.

The Romanesque chancel also had a vaulted roof but it collapsed in the 15th century. Was it a Benedictine chancel with two spans and two side aisles leading into the apse? Or, as a miniature in the Heures du Duc de Berry would seem to suggest, did the chancel have an ambulatory?

The north wall of the Romanesque nave (12th century)

The nave in Mont Saint-Michel minster shows the progress made in architecture during the Romanesque period. Thereafter, the solidity of the building was based on a framework of pillars and arches rather than on a huge pile of stone. Weight and thrust were taken into consideration. "The entire building then becomes an active organism, not a passive force. A piece of masonry becomes a piece of architecture" (Germain Bazin).

This slenderness, elegance and regularity were not achieved without disasters. One morning in 1103, while the monks were at prayer, the north wall of the nave collapsed onto the monastery buildings. It had to be rebuilt, thicker and with fewer openings. The south section of the nave, then, dates from the 11th century while the north wall is 12th century.

Nave of the church.
Photo Bertrand Dauleux.

Romanesque art

Only in the 19th century was the notion of "Romanesque" art accepted. Until then, everything was called "gothic", not without contempt at that. As many buildings in Normandy had been constructed from the 11th century onwards, the scholars first spoke of "Norman art"; then, to characterise an artistic movement that stretched beyond the Norman frontiers, historians preferred the notion of "Romanesque" art, with respect to the Romanic language, which was the result of Latin's evolution through its' contact with the invaders' languages. As Richard II, duke of Normandy, had positioned an Italian, Guillaume de Volpiano, in Fécamp. The latter reorganised Norman monasteries, made the duchy a training site for bishops and abbots, and favoured the reconstruction of the buildings. His influence was essential for the unity of Romanesque art in the whole of Normandy.

In each span, three storeys are marked out by horizontal banding – the great arches, the triforium above, and the clerestorey at the top which lets in the light. Each span is topped by a large relieving arch. By bearing all the weight of the rafters, this arch enabled the builder to raise only a thin wall between the pillars. The other unusual feature is the long engaged pillar which rises to the very top of the church, forming a veritable "inner buttress".

The pillars in the chancel (mid 15th century)

When the pillars in the chancel reached gallery level, the work was stopped and it did not begin again until the early 16th century. These ten pillars gave the chancel a polygonal layout. Each pillar is shaped like a diamond and consists of a sheaf of colonettes, all of them similar in appearance. Each colonette corresponds to one base of the ogival vaulting or arches. All these details create a sense of organic logic in this perfect example of architecture at its best. An ambulatory runs round the chancel, with radiating chapels. At the end of the church, in the chapel behind the High Altar, is a piscina, decorated with floral motifs. It was designed to hold holy water. The chapel was known in the 17th century as Notre-Dame-du-Circuit, the "circuit" being the ambulatory.

The Flamboyant Gothic Chancel (1450-1521)

Its design was based on the nave in St. Ouen's Abbey in Rouen where Guillaume d'Estouteville was also Abbot. The original plans may have been drawn up by the same architect, Guillaume Pontis. St. Ouen's was considered in the late Middle Ages as one of the finest examples

Cross section of the transept.

of Gothic architecture then in existence. The 15th-century project for the Mont was scrupulously adhered to, although the building work was completed by Guillaume and Jean de Lamps in the early 16th century. Four centuries, then, separate the Romanesque nave and the chancel that may be seen as a final expression of mediaeval architecture.

Everything has been sacrificed to the sense of verticality. The pillars are devoid of capitals. The narrowness of the arches in comparison to their height emphasises the impression of an upward vertical swing. Each span is also broken up by three storeys i.e. the arches, the triforium or blind storey, and the clerestorey.

The triforium

The triforium, which is supported by the pillars in the ambulatory, skirts the pillars to avoid weakening them. The openwork in the gallery lets light flood in. Flamboyant Gothic architecture turned this into a fine piece of stone tracery with a balustrade over three-lobed arches and numerous lancets (elongated ogival arches) topped by a frieze. The ogival arches top the « glass cage » as F. Enaud termed the top of the chancel. They are interconnected by keystones bearing the coats-of-arms of the abbey, Jean Le Veneur, and St. Michael slaying the dragon.

The lace staircase

A staircase was built in one pier on the chevet that was thicker than the others. It leads to a walkway high above the ground, connected to the roof of the chancel. The Flamboyant Gothic style demanded that the granite of the handrail and the finialed pinnacles be traceried. Through this piece of lacework carved in stone, there is a superb view right across Mont Saint-Michel Bay with its sandbanks and pools of water.

The chevet (early 16th century)

The unusually high vaulting in the chancel had a tendency to lean outwards and it had, therefore, to be counterbalanced. Flying buttresses were used as stone props. Oblique forces are transmitted to enormous vertical buttresses, made up of two piers that are veritable aerial pillars, joined by a wall with tracery at the top and coping above it. The piers rest on the dividing walls in the radiating chapels and are therefore laid out in a fan shape. If the chevet as we see it is a "forest of stone", it is because prudence had become the architect's watchword for fear of further catastrophe.

The piers around the chevet are topped by pinnacles, pyramids ornamented with stone flowers that bear witness to the decorative genius of the period.

The chancel ambulatory.

The flamboyant apse.

The monks' walkway (12th century). Photo Richard Nourry.

The Romanesque abbey buildings and crypts

In the Romanesque period (11th century), the abbey entrance lay on the north-west side of the rock. The buildings consisted of three storeys, with the dorter beside the church situated above the monks' gallery that was itself built on top of the Aquilon Chamber.

The abbot, Robert de Thorigny, had his lodgings built on the west side.

The minster is supported by crypts such as Our Lady of the Thirty Candles (Notre-Dame des Trente Cierges) which lies beneath the north arm of the transept. This chapel, where the Virgin Mary's clothes were once kept, was the spiritual heart of the abbey. The vestibule has a central pillar decorated with Gothic foliage and was once used as a prison. In those days, it was known as the "Devil's Dungeon".

The monks' gallery (12th century)

This long chamber beneath the dorter represents a turning-point in architectural design. Roger II originally had groined arches built but Bernard du Bec had them replaced by ogival arching after a fire in 1138. Two arches set between transverse ribs cross each other diagonally. This technique, which gives the vaulting greater fullness, is a forerunner of Gothic architecture. The two aisles separated by five pillars stand above the rock to the east and the Aquilon Chamber to the west.

Nobody knows what the chamber was originally intended to be used for. Tradition has it that this was the Romanesque cloister where the monks relaxed and took a stroll, hence its name. The adjoining buildings, which have been mutilated, are said to have been the refectory and kitchen. The Maurists turned them into latrines.

The Aquilon room (12th century)

The name of an icy blast was given to the Romanesque almonry because it lay on the north side of the rock. Since the original entrance to the abbey was on the north-west side, it was in this room that pilgrims were welcomed to the Mont. It was not connected to the monastery buildings in order to prevent any disruption to the solitude of the brothers. This means that the staircase leading to the monks' gallery is a more recent addition.

After the fire of 1112, Abbot Roger II had the wooden roof replaced by stone vaulting, in an effort to decrease the fire hazard. The vaulting is groined and is

The Aquilon room
(or Roman chaplaincy).
Photo Richard Nourry.

The construction

One only needs to walk through the Mounts' abbey to realise that the monks had chosen this site not only to mark their severance from the world, but also because they wished to take the challenge to raise there an ensemble of constructions to astonish man and honour God, for the construction of a great church and monastic buildings on a steep rock was seemingly attempting the impossible. Underground chapels and crypts bore the nave of the sanctuary, which was flanked at the north by a three-level building, and by another ensemble at the west. Only then did The Wonder become a spectacular architectural ensemble for the monks. There were of course accidents, in time: walls or vaults fell down, but the monument survived. Stability was based on the successful dialogue between the monastic community, who expressed its' visions, the architects – they are unknown to us, and were very likely monks themselves – and the craftsmen. Stones had to be brought to the Mount. Then, following the plans that had been suggested, stone cutters prepared the stones so that they would be perfectly adjusted. Timber frameworks were raised to support the arches. Wheels enabled the craftsmen to hoist the stones that were then set into place, and the timber structures were then withdrawn once the general balance had been attained.

Notre-Dame-sous-Terre.

ment here, and meted out punishment here. On the upper floor, beneath the platform at the West Front of the minster, were two rooms designed for the Abbot's Court. When the Mont was used as a prison, the famous "iron cage" used to be hung from the 11th-century barrel vaulting. Robert de Thorigny commissioned the building of his austere apartments further west, in the 12th century. They looked out to sea and it was here that he received a visit from the King, Henri II, in 1158. On the lower storey near the door was the gatehouse. The porter could keep a watchful eye on travellers passing beneath the porch beyond the canopy near the Aquilon Chamber. Two dungeons, nicknamed "Vade in pace", were built into the ground here when the abbey was turned into the "Bastille of the Sea". They were known familiarly as the "twins".

Notre-Dame-sous-Terre (mid 10th century)

Notre-Dame-sous-Terre is the Preromanesque church. It was built in the middle of the 10th century, at the same time as the abbey was founded. Its two parallel aisles are separated by a wall consisting of two arches. Carolingian traditions are apparent in several places. The Cyclopean wall at the end of the chapel may be a throwback to the former oratory dating from the 8th and 9th centuries. The church, which originally stood in the open air, became a crypt when the Romanesque nave was built above it. It was badly damaged in the 18th century then restored in the 20th. Prestressed

formed by the penetration of two barrel vaults within the same semicircle. The austere capitals are decorated with swirls and a central heart-shaped motif.

Robert de Thorigny's apartments (late 12th century)

Pilgrims arriving at the Mont followed long vaulted galleries to the south side of the abbey. The Romanesque abbot's lodgings stood at the south-west and were three storeys high. This was the seat of temporal life in the monastery. The Abbot lived here, welcomed visitors here, passed judge-

concrete was used to bear the weight of the minster above.

The wheel, the hoist (19th century) and the Romanesque ossuary

The Romanesque abbey was extended on the south side by buildings designed to accommodate pilgrims but the three storeys collapsed in 1817. The only reminder of them these days is a model kept in the Invalides Museum. The infirmary opened onto St. Stephen's Chapel, the mortuary chapel where, it is thought, cadavers may have been laid out. It had 13th-century ogival vaulting. The monks' ossuary was next to the chapel. Death, then, was an integral part of the architecture. The prison service installed a huge wheel in this ossuary and prisoners walked inside it to make it turn. A trolley would then be drawn up along a hoist, a veritable stone ladder snaking its way up the wall of rock.

It was, in fact, a reminder of the Middle Ages since it resembled the wheel used by the monks. One of them was in use for many years in the Romanesque undercroft and there was a second one in the Gothic undercroft in the Marvel. It was this latter system which was used by a captain during the Wars of Religion in his attempt to enter the citadel.

The foal.

The wheel.

The Saint Martin chapel.

rous austerity. The Christian liturgy preferred crypts, which were places of meditation and prayer.

The stone vaulting was the most important feature of the mediaeval architecture. The dim atmosphere was particularly well-suited to the funeral rites to which the abbey devoted itself. The noblemen of the day preferred to be laid to rest in the shade of a church. The vaulting also improved the acoustics. And, after all, plainsong was the monks' only passion. Indeed, it may arguably have been their supreme contribution to the arts.

The Crypt of the Mighty Pillars (1446-1450)

The Romanesque chancel collapsed in 1421 but war made rebuilding impossible. Once peace had been restored, Cardinal d'Estouteville, the influential abbot of the Mont, ordered the work to begin. The Crypt of the Mighty Pillars (Crypte des Gros Piliers) was erected in only a few years and was designed to support the new chancel. Ten enormous cylindrical columns were built, perhaps around the original Romanesque pillars. Two of them, which are smaller than the others, were given the descriptive name "palm trees". Prism-shaped ribs bring life to the vaulting, penetrating the pillars or walls at their base. Flamboyant Gothic architecture imposed its skilful techniques and its sense of aesthetics with the art of carving voussoirs (stones in vaulted roofs carved in the shape of a corner) and the precise adjustment of the stonework allied to a preference for sharp, rather than rounded, forms.

The Saint Martin chapel

The St. Martin crypt bears the weight of the south transept of the abbey church. Its semicircular barrel vaulting is a model of rigou-

The Large Pillars crypt. Photo Richard Nourry.

The Marvel

The "Marvel" is the Gothic part of the abbey. It was built after the abbey was destroyed in the early years of the 13th century, replacing the Romanesque monastery buildings which had become too small and were totally lacking in amenities. The view here shows the east wing, the first to be built. Above a wide bank, there are three storeys symbolising the social hierarchy of the Middle Ages. The poor were given food on the lowest storey, in the almonry where the groined vaulting was reminiscent of traditional Romanesque architecture. On the second storey, the abbot welcomed rich, influential visitors, in the Guests' Chamber, where the vaulting is ogival. Finally, the refectory was the monks' dining hall - and the clergy were considered to take priority over all other members of society in mediaeval times. Wooden rafters were selected for this chamber in order to avoid weakening the building as a whole. The building was supported by massive external piers.

The western section of the Marvel was built after the east wing and had three storeys. At the top were the cloisters, beneath them was the Knights' Chamber with its huge bay window, and below that was the undercroft which was used as a cellar. Supplies were heaved up from the sand below by means of a great wheel. A drawbridge had been slung between two massive buttresses that supported the building on the north side. This wing

The cloister.

of the abbey was reserved for the brothers, and formed the backcloth to their monastic life. It was intended to build a third group of buildings even further west, to include the chapter house where the community would hold its meetings and assemblies but the project was abandoned. At the most inaccessible spot, in the north-west corner, was the charter-room where the monastery archives were kept, proof of its wealth and its past heritage. This small airy room stands on top of an enormous corner pier.

The cloisters
(early 13th century)

This was the place for exercise, conversation and meditation. It forms the top floor of the Marvel and it was reserved for the monks. The garth, which seems to hang in midair between the sea below and the sky above, is surrounded by covered walkways. It lies on the same level as the refectory and the church and rests on the vaulting in the Knights' Chamber. In order to lay out this area, which was both open and enclosed, the north transept of the abbey church was shortened at the spot where a huge Gothic window was built. The lavatorium, or lavabo, was built here with a double bench and a fountain, all at ground level. The abbot would celebrate the ceremony of the Washing of the Feet here, in memory of Christ. The monks also washed here before meals. Originally, the western gallery was intended to open onto the chapter house but it was never built. What would have been the doorways to the chapter house are now three bay windows.

The colonettes in the cloisters

The shafts may have been carved in England and imported into France. Originally, they were probably made of a fine-grained limestone similar to marble. But the architect, Corroyer, preferred a fine-grained granite. The hardness of this stone explains the prismatic outline and the simplicity of the plinths, bases and abaci. The colonettes were placed in staggered lines i.e. instead of being in pairs, they are in two rows that are slightly out of line with each other. They are connected by arches along the same two rows, and "diagonal" arches mark out small triangular vaults. This succession of tripods gives the building absolute stability, since the weight and load are regularly distributed. The technique, which was quite unknown in cloisters before this date, was nevertheless fairly commonplace in Norman Gothic architecture where it was frequently incorporated into doorways. As this style of architecture did not lend itself to empty spaces, large crochets decorated with foliage were carved beneath the arches.

A squinch in the cloisters

Between the arches in the cloisters, the soft Caen limestone squinches have been ornamented with carvings, fairly conclusive proof, if any was needed, of the extent to which Norman architecture was fond of stone tracery. Two designs were chosen i.e. a rose surrounded by three other smaller roses, and a leaf pattern that fills the enti-

The restoration

Paradoxically, the monastery was maybe saved due to the purpose it served as a prison, which made its' maintenance remain necessary when the monastic community disappeared. But the prison authorities adapted the buildings to their needs. Nonetheless, such a convents' architectural interest became increasingly apparent as the romantic artists rediscovered the middle ages. Simultaneously, politicians, administrators and historians grew aware of the importance of saving endangered historical monuments. Saving often meant recreating, and this was no easy task, firstly because documents were often missing, and secondly because the Mount's edifices had evolved in time. As they allied imagination to rationality, the architects who followed each other with the task of saving and restoring the Mount drew this strange silhouette that all know.

Decorated corner pieces.

A garden suspended between sea and sky...
Photo Richard Nourry.

The Marvel -
longitudinal sectional view over the east building.
Drawing by Emile Sagot, pen and water coulour, circa 1865.
© CNMHS.

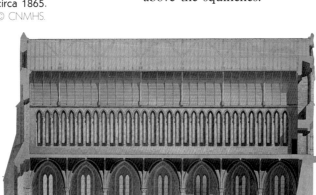

re triangular section. The plant theme predominated, especially the vine, because it gave great scope for the sculptor's imagination. The cavity carved out in the wall provides a dark background from which the swirls of the carvings stand out. A frieze runs along the cloister walls above the squinches.

The refectory
(early 13th century)

Monastic meals were veritable ceremonials. It took major feats of technical skill to embellish the room in which they were taken. Setting aside any question of a vaulted ceiling which would probably have been too heavy, the architects preferred to erect semi-circular rafters, a huge upturned hull built in the Gothic period but that was nevertheless reminiscent of the nave in the Romanesque part of the church. A thick wall bore this continual weight and, in order to avoid weakening it with huge bays, narrow windows scarcely wider than slits were built. Set deep in the walls, they are invisible from the entrance to the refectory although they provide an astonishing amount of light. Each of them is flanked by slender colonettes. Meals were taken in silence while one of the monks aloud read from holy texts. The pulpit stands in the south wall and, thanks to the excellent acoustics, the entire chamber was filled with his voice. The cellarer's office and kitchen were on the south side of the refectory.

The Guests's Chamber
(early 13th century)

Built by Abbot Raoul des Isles, this chamber *(Salle des Hôtes)* was intended for rich or famous visitors who took their meals here with the abbot. Two aisles in which the tables were set out, two huge fireplaces where the meals were prepared and which were

THE EASTERN BUILDING

separated from the rest of the chamber by tapestries, and latrines in the north wall – these were the necessary "mod. cons." in any reception room of the day. The elegance of the ogival arches and pillars, the light flooding in through the great east-facing bay windows, the beauty of the stylised foliage, and the other decorative features that have since disappeared (paintings, tiling, stained glass, and tapestries) all made Gothic architecture a means of displaying enormous wealth. Using a style that originated in the Paris Basin, this chamber was "one of the most elegant creations of vernacular architecture in the Middle Ages" (Germain Bazin) and was a forerunner of Royaumont and Ourscamp. The Guests' Chamber is preceded on the south side by the Chapel of St. Madeleine where travellers prayed both before and after meals.

The Knights' Chamber (early 13th century)

The chamber (*Salle des Chevaliers*) owes its name to the order of chivalry instituted by Louis XI, the Knights of St. Michael. Yet it seems that no meeting was ever held here. This was, in fact, the "calefactory". Huge fireplaces, with a mantelpiece rising to the roof, afforded some protection against the cold. Tapestries divided the chamber off into small rooms. They also hid the raised passageway to the south, along which guests went on their way to the church without disturbing the monks. The chamber was also the "main work room", the scriptorium, a quite different place to the ordinary calefactory in Benedictine monasteries. It

UPPER LEVEL OF THE MARVEL: monk's refectory.

MIDDLE LEVEL: guests room.

LOWER LEVEL: the gothic chaplaincy.

THE WESTERN BUILDING

UPPER LEVEL OF THE MARVEL: the cloister.

MIDDLE LEVEL: the guests room.

LOWER LEVEL: the wine cellar

was here that the monks copied and illuminated manuscripts.

The originality of Norman architecture comes to the fore here. It is sturdiness, rather than elegance, which prevails, and the development in design ideas is quite obvious when this chamber is compared to the Guests' Chamber built in an earlier period. Here, the pillars are stocky and the outline of the ogival vaulting is more noticeable. The torus, the major piece of moulding, is set off by two deep grooves. Lastly, the almost vertical capitals are decorated with fine carvings of foliage.

The abbot's lodging

The abbot lived in close proximity to the pilgrims, while the monks sought peace in the "enclosure" on the north side. The various parts of the abbey can be "read" from right to left, i.e. from East to South. Beyond the Marvel and the forework are the abbey lodgings, the "worldly" part of the abbey, built in stages between the 13th and 16th centuries. The Courtroom lies above the Guardroom. Known as Belle-Chaise, it has narrow windows separated by colonettes. The garrison was billetted in the Perrine Tower, a massive square construction with a pointed roof built by Pierre le Roi. This tower is immediately adjacent to the residence occupied by the Bailiff, a lay officer within the community.
Beyond it were the

WESTERN BUILD-
ING CROSS
SECTION

Abbot's apartments, in an impressive residence supported by three piers and four relieving arches. During the days of the monarchy, political prisoners were detained here, in Minor and Major Exile. Finally, there is the Chapel of St. Catherine of the Steps *(Sainte-Catherine-des-Degrés)* and the last building, the Priory, near Gautier's Leap. This architecture may be vernacular but it also had decidedly military strength. Danger was rife and the life of the abbey had to be protected at all costs.

The abbot's apartments.

The "Belle-Chaise" court room.

Belle-Chaise

Above the Guardroom lay "Belle-Chaise", the Abbot's courtroom. It was here that he passed judgement, for he had the right to sentence anybody on his land. The only exceptions to this rule were criminal offences, for a man of the cloth was forbidden to spill blood. The Abbot sat on a throne, the chair or "chaise" which gave the chamber its name.

The abbot's apartments.

The town of Mont-Saint-Michel and its ramparts

The town

Mont Saint-Michel is also a "town" or, to be more precise, a small Norman village nestling at the foot of the abbey with which it has always been closely connected. The first houses were built on the north side ; later, they huddled on the south side. Pilgrims would then find inns and taverns awaiting them, just as today's visitors find hotels and restaurants. They bought badges of pilgrimage just as tourists buy souvenirs. A narrow street leads up to the monastery. A shortcut called the Chemin des Monteux was preferred by the locals, the Montois. A tiny church dedicated to St. Peter welcomes the faithful. A fine carving of the head of Christ, commissioned by André de Laure in 1483, is now kept in the sacristy. A small cemetery watched over by a gra-

View of the abbey from the east, with the Belle-Chaise court room.
Photo Eric Cattin.

The abbey behind the ramparts.

The Artichokes House.

The Mermaid's House.

For the Mother Poulard's famous omelette.

nite Cross stands high above the sea close to the church. A few of the old houses have been preserved e.g. the 15th-century Hôtellerie de la Lycorne (the Unicorn Hostelry); others have been restored like the house said to have belonged to Tiphaine Raguenel, Du Guesclin's wife. Others have been built in a style considered to be appropriate.

The ramparts

In the 15th century, walls were erected right around the town. They were supported by towers, starting on the north side with its watchtower (a corbelled stone lookout post facing the shoreline) round to the town gates. There are obvious signs of progress when these towers are compared to the techniques used in earlier times, during the Middle Ages. In the meantime, the system of defence had beco-

me of vital importance. The towers were no longer miniature fortresses built to deal with minor local uprisings. Interconnected by a parapet walk, they no longer overlooked the town walls ; on the contrary, it was the walls that defended the towers. This is the principle

The Ramparts cafe.
Collection of postcards from the Avranches Library.

Coat of arms
by Robert Jolivet.

behind modern-day thinking viz "whatever provides the defence must itself be defended" (Germain Bazin). The ramparts, with their numerous projections, run close by the houses in the village, with machicolations at intervals from which the defending forces could rain projectiles down on the enemy. The Buckle Tower was once known as a small bastion. It juts out over the sand like a spur of rock and its shape is a forerunner of the fortifications built by Vauban. The horizontal slit windows were designed for bombards, the enormous late-mediaeval cannon. As a town surrounded by walls was virtually impregnable, progress had been made in artillery and methods of attack.

The Hayloft and
the Gabriel tower (1524)

It was the king's lieutenant, Gabriel Dupuy, who completed the Mont's system of defence. And indeed at the beginning of the 16th century, the skill of the military engineer was almost at the peak of perfection, as is obvious from the Gabriel Tower. All possible angles of fire were catered for. The garrison could take action against any attack with all due speed. The cannon were set up inside the thick walls. The large bastion, which is reminiscent of the ones in Fougères Castle, defended the entrance to the hayloft. A chimney provided an outlet for the smoke. In the 17th century, a windmill was built on the platform.

The Fanils warehouse
and the Gabriel tower.

The Mont Saint-Michel at night.

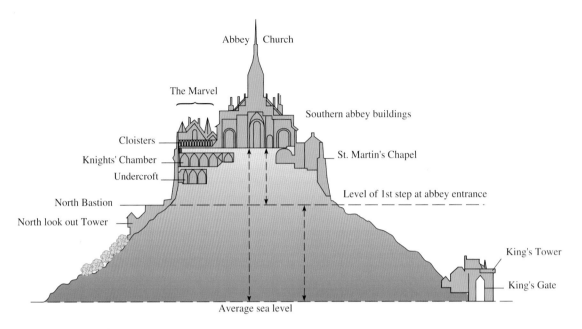

Abbey Church

The Marvel

Southern abbey buildings

Cloisters

Knights' Chamber

Undercroft

St. Martin's Chapel

Level of 1st step at abbey entrance

North Bastion

North look out Tower

King's Tower

King's Gate

Average sea level

North-South cros-section

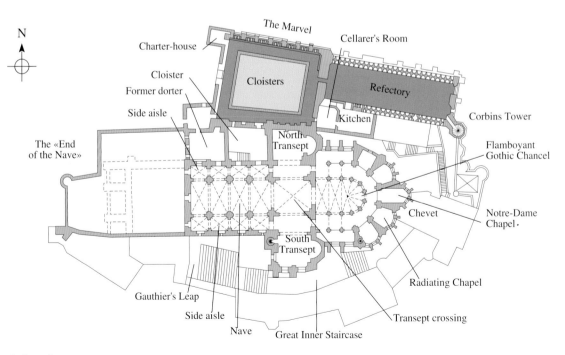

N

The Marvel

Charter-house

Cellarer's Room

Cloister

Former dorter

Cloisters

Refectory

Side aisle

Kitchen

Corbins Tower

The «End of the Nave»

North Transept

Flamboyant Gothic Chancel

Chevet

Notre-Dame Chapel

South Transept

Radiating Chapel

Gauthier's Leap

Side aisle

Transept crossing

Nave

Great Inner Staircase

Church Level

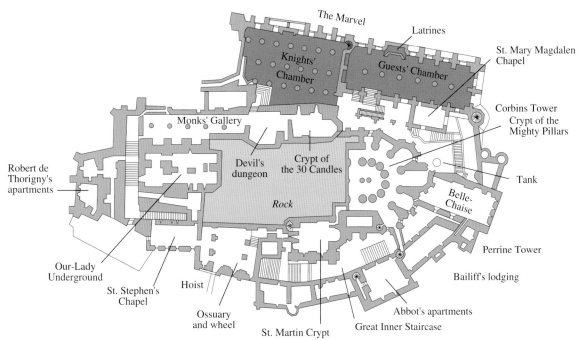

The Marvel
Latrines
Knights' Chamber
Guests' Chamber
St. Mary Magdalen Chapel
Corbins Tower
Crypt of the Mighty Pillars
Monks' Gallery
Devil's dungeon
Crypt of the 30 Candles
Tank
Robert de Thorigny's apartments
Belle-Chaise
Rock
Perrine Tower
Our-Lady Underground
Bailiff's lodging
St. Stephen's Chapel
Hoist
Ossuary and wheel
St. Martin Crypt
Great Inner Staircase
Abbot's apartments

Intermediate level

The Marvel
Abbey walls
Plants, Gardens
Rock

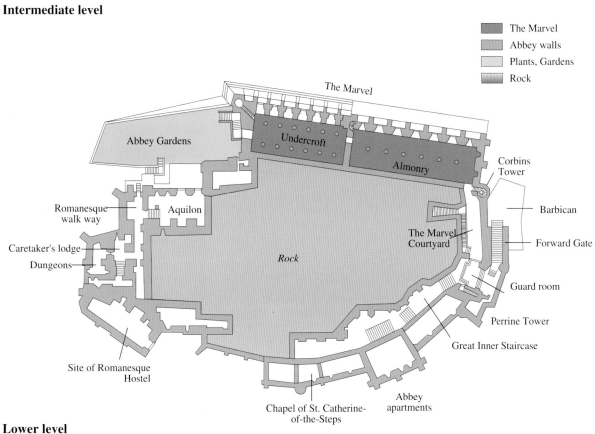

The Marvel
Abbey Gardens
Undercroft
Almonry
Corbins Tower
Romanesque walk way
Aquilon
Barbican
Caretaker's lodge
The Marvel Courtyard
Forward Gate
Dungeons
Rock
Guard room
Perrine Tower
Great Inner Staircase
Site of Romanesque Hostel
Chapel of St. Catherine-of-the-Steps
Abbey apartments

Lower level

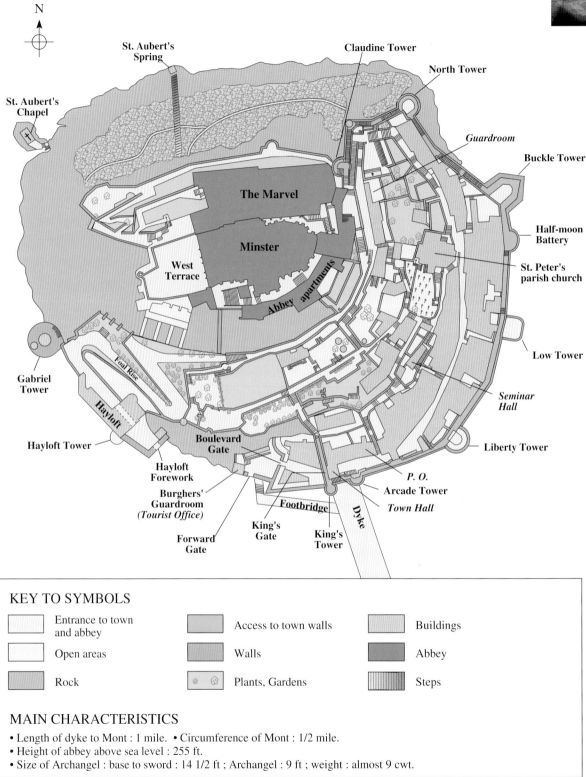

KEY TO SYMBOLS

- Entrance to town and abbey
- Open areas
- Rock
- Access to town walls
- Walls
- Plants, Gardens
- Buildings
- Abbey
- Steps

MAIN CHARACTERISTICS

- Length of dyke to Mont : 1 mile. • Circumference of Mont : 1/2 mile.
- Height of abbey above sea level : 255 ft.
- Size of Archangel : base to sword : 14 1/2 ft ; Archangel : 9 ft ; weight : almost 9 cwt.

Cover page: The Mont Saint Michel – view from the south-east.

Cet ouvrage a été imprimé par POLLINA à Luçon (85) - n° 76838-A.
I.S.B.N. 2.7373.2251.0 - Dépôt légal : mars 1999
N° éditeur : 3639.01.06.03.99